CW00496036

Touched by
RESURRECTION
LOVE

TREVOR HUDSON

STRUIK CHRISTIAN BOOKS

TOUCHED BY RESURRECTION LOVE

Struik Christian Books Ltd

A division of New Holland Publishing (South Africa) (Pty) Ltd
(New Holland Publishing is a member of Johnnic Communications Ltd)
Cornelis Struik House
80 McKenzie Street
Cape Town 8001

Reg. No. 1971/00972/07

Edited by Jenny Crickmore-Thompson
DTP by Louise Fouché
Cover design by Christian Jaggers
Cover photograph by Photo Access and Getty Images
Cover reproduction by Hirt & Carter Cape (Pty) Ltd
Printed and bound by Paarl Print
Oosterland Street, Paarl, South Africa.

ISBN 1 86823 671 4

www.struikchristianbooks.co.za

To Debbie, Joni and Mark

Acknowledgements

I want to express my gratitude to the folk at Struik Christian Books, who continue to encourage my writing efforts. Thank you to Fiona Lee, Veronica Language and their team for making this book a reality.

Thank you to fellow pilgrim Bill Meaker for his patient reading of each chapter and his helpful comments. I am also indebted to Lyn Meyer for preparing the manuscript for publication.

It is an honour to have Dallas Willard write the foreword. Over the years his friendship and writings have profoundly shaped my understanding of what it means to follow Jesus. Thank you also to Peter Storey for commenting on the book in such a personal way.

How do I say thank you to Debbie, my partner in marriage, and to our children, Joni and Mark? Our life together is the greatest gift I have been given. God is indeed good, gracious and generous.

Finally, I thank the Risen Lord for his faithful companionship in each moment of my life. I pray that He will use these words to help others find hope beyond their tears.

Trevor Hudson
November 2003

Contents

Foreword

Trevor Hudson is remarkably gifted at unrolling the contents of a scriptural story right into the midst of your life. He is an open soul – something learned through a long spiritual process in his life – who is able to open other souls. Yours and mine. This is our profound need: for our souls to be opened. To turn loose the inner bondages by which we shut ourselves in, away from others and from God. We have been hurt. There we think to be safe. There we die alone. Who can help us?

The opening of a soul comes through little cracks and progresses slowly. We are such beings as can only let go of our inner hold in response to grace – true gift, no strings. Grace gently suggests to us that good is present and coming towards us. This is perceived through a tiny crack in our armour. Could we widen that crack just a bit, get a slightly better view? Perhaps begin to let the gift enter our shell, just a little? Perhaps we could begin by spending some time quietly resting in solitude and silence.

The stories of Jesus are the primary overtures of grace in a world that knows little of true gift. We can let them in. Indeed, they are so winsome, who can keep them out once they appear? They are like raindrops and sunshine, and the flowers in our soul begin to grow. Without our knowing how, without our even intending it. We begin to find good we did not expect or hope for: here, there, in the world, in others. In ourselves, can it be? We ask: 'Who has done this?' And we find that Jesus Himself came in with the stories.

Meditation is turning to the gift of Jesus. Waiting before it. Paying attention. Letting things be what they are. Finding we have a soul. Suspecting that we are an unceasing spiritual being with an eternal destiny in the world of a good God. Meditation itself proves to be a gift in retrospect.

At first Mary 'did not know it was Jesus'. Thought He was the gardener! What we learn in meditation upon Christ is from another world, but does not demand understanding at the outset. Just longing from the heart. Mary had that. You probably do too. So make space for it, and take this book as a guide. Just follow the instructions given by the author. Let the words wash over you. They will do the work. You can count on it.

Dallas Willard

Introduction

For just over three decades I have worked as a pastor in a local congregation. It has been a huge privilege. These years have made me deeply aware of the depth and extent of human trauma, bereavement, anxiety and emotional pain that lies all around us and also in our own hearts. Nearly everyone carries a heavy burden. Perhaps you do too. If you do, I would like to offer you these meditations on one of my favourite Easter stories – the encounter between the Risen Christ and Mary Magdalene.

It is a deeply moving story of the transformation and hope that can lie beyond our tears. It begins with Mary standing outside the tomb where Jesus had been buried after his crucifixion. She is brokenhearted and weeping. Her whole world has collapsed. But her story does not end here. It closes with her running to find the other disciples with the incredible news that Christ was alive. Her darkest night had suddenly been changed into brightest day. She had experienced the transforming power of the resurrection for herself. She had become a person of Easter faith living in a Good Friday world.

This transforming experience has become a reality for countless people throughout the centuries and still happens

today. The Risen Christ continues to meet with us at the point
of our deepest need. As He came to Mary 2 000 years ago,
so He comes to us in our dark and difficult places. Sometimes, like Mary herself, we do not recognise Him immediately. But as we open our hearts and our minds to his living
presence, and to the message of his resurrection, we find ourselves gradually empowered to live beyond our tears, to go
out and connect with those suffering around us.

Another reason for writing this book has been to encourage others to really *live* in a gospel story. It is so easy to
turn Bible reading into a mere intellectual exercise. This
happens whenever we read the Bible without being touched
and transformed by what we read. We gain more informa-
tion, but we remain the same. Through these meditations I
want to show you how we can stay with a gospel story for a
few weeks and allow it to permeate our entire life. When
we do this, we begin to experience the resurrection power
of the Christian message to overcome sorrow with joy,
darkness with light, defeat with victory.

As you read this book, may I encourage you to do so
meditatively. My suggestion is that you take a few days to
read each chapter, allowing five to ten minutes after each
reading to reflect on what you've read. You may wish to ask
yourself, 'What thoughts crossed my mind, and what feel-

ings did I experience as I read this chapter?' You will notice that there is space for you to record your reflections.

It would be even better to read this book with one or
two friends, or in a small group. Each week you could get
together, share your reflections and learn from each other's
experiences. Our journey in faith is always a journey together. I have also offered three questions at the end of
each chapter that will help you to relate better to what you
have read, along with a prayer that you can use each day. I
have called this prayer a 'breath-prayer', because I hope
that praying it will become second nature to you.

Let me end this introduction by offering you a prayer
that you might like to pray before you begin this book. It
was written by a very dear friend whose life was a living
expression of the resurrection. His resurrection faith helped
him to overcome a terrible depression, to live through the
death of one of his children and to shape his life into a powerful channel of God's love and care. Here is the prayer:

> I ask You, life-giving and victorious, resurrected
> Jesus, to help me to grasp the full meaning of your
> victory over suffering, death and evil; and to help
> me live with hope and love, with joy and expecta-
> tion, with patience and determination, with con-

fidence and peace as I prepare for the transcendent fellowship of eternity that You have opened to me by your death and resurrection. May I now know something of the kingdom for which You told me to pray and then know its fullness by growing forever in your loving presence.

Morton Kelsey

May these meditations open your heart and mind to be touched by Resurrection Love.

CHAPTER I

Befriending our tears

Befriending our tears

But Mary stood weeping outside the tomb. As she
wept, she bent over to look into the tomb, and
she saw two angels in white, sitting where the body
of Jesus had been lying, one at the head and the
other at the feet. (John 20:11)

It was the late seventies and I was sitting with Gordon
Cosby, co-founder and pastor of the Church of the Sa-
viour, a small, vibrant, ecumenical congregation in the
inner city of Washington. We were having lunch in the
Potter's House, one of the church's many ministries serv-
ing the city, and reflecting on the challenges of preaching
within the contemporary urban context. Almost forty years
of servant ministry had given my lunch companion a pro-

found pastoral wisdom. When I asked him whether he had anything to say to me about sharing the Gospel on the suffering continent of Africa, he responded, 'Always remember that each person you see in the congregation sits next to his or her own pool of tears.'

I have never forgotten these words. Nearly every time I stand to share the good news from God with others this sentence comes into my mind. The words always remind me of the suffering present amongst those gathered together. It has been a difficult awareness from which to preach and teach. There are times when I am deeply concerned that my words will come across as glib, or superficial or perhaps even empty. Even as I write this meditation I am aware of these possibilities. Certainly Gordon's words to me have increased my discomfort with any kind of spiritual talk that overlooks the pain that people experience.

Each of us does sit next to a pool of tears. As you read my words you are sitting beside your pool, and as I write these words, I am seated next to mine. Our pools are different. Some are deeper, some are muddier. Some have been caused by what has been done to us; some are the result of our own doing. These pools remind us of the grief and losses that we have experienced through our lives. It might have been the death of a loved one, the pain of divorce, abuse as a child, the unmet longing for a partner, the loss of a job or a rejection by a close friend. There are so many different kinds of pools – the list goes on and on.

But tears don't have to end in sadness and pain. As different as our 'pools of tears' may be, they can lead us into a new space of change and growth. If our tears are allowed to tell their stories, they can become the means by which our lives are transformed. Whether they flow down our cheeks, or represent our cry for help, the silent needs of our grieving and broken hearts, our tears can become the agents of resurrection and newness. This is what we will learn when we think more deeply about the encounter between the risen Jesus and Mary Magdalene, on that first Easter Sunday morning.

Let us begin to explore this meeting. It is a story about the journey to transformation that lies beyond tears. When we find Mary standing outside the tomb, she is weeping. Two days ago, she had seen the person whom she loved dearly, the one who had released her from her torment, put to death on a cross. No doubt his death had left her confused, numb, desperate. Ever since the initial encounter when Jesus had freed her (Luke 8:2), her whole life had revolved around Him. She had followed him around Galilee. She had been at the foot of the cross, and accompa-

nied his crucified body to the tomb in Joseph's garden.
Then early on Sunday morning she had gone with a small
group of women to the tomb. To their great distress, the
stone had been rolled away. Not only was the tomb open,
the body of Jesus was gone. Soon afterwards Peter and
John arrived, only to depart and leave Mary alone in the
garden, standing beside her pool of tears.

The longer I think about Mary's tears, the more I believe it was necessary for her to cry. She needed those
tears to express the deep grief of her heart. They were
necessary to ease the intensity of her inner pain. They were
necessary to relax those raw nerves rapidly reaching breaking point. They were necessary to lighten the weight of
sorrow bearing heavily down upon her spirit. They were
necessary for the processes of healing and transformation
to begin. Indeed, I venture to believe that, without her
tears, she may have failed to recognise the shining figures
inside the tomb. After all, tears can help us to see things
differently. They clear the dust from our eyes, and give us
fresh insight and vision.

Her tears also remind us that it is human to cry. Some
of us, especially men, need this reminder. Often we feel
uncomfortable about our tears. Over the years I have been
at many funerals where I have witnessed heartbroken mourn-

ers, struggling to hold back tears, almost as if they were
not appropriate. Earlier today I sat with a young man in his
mid-thirties, who, as he told me the story of his marriage
breaking up, began to cry. Reaching for a tissue from the
table between us, he apologised. 'I'm sorry for breaking
down like this,' he said as he blew his nose, 'I really need to
get a grip on myself.' How different it was for Mary in her
personal pain and grief – she seemed to know that tears
were an intimate part of what it means to be a human
being in pain. We need to learn from her.

Today I invite you to glimpse the promise hidden in your
pool of tears. It is the promise of new beginnings. One way
to do this would be to become quiet for a few moments and
to imaginatively join Mary as she stands weeping outside the
tomb. See yourself meeting Mary in the garden, her eyes
and yours filled with tears. Go together across to the open
tomb, look inside, and slowly take in what you see. Witness
the intriguing emptiness of the grave ... the grave clothes
neatly folded ... the shroud and napkin lying separately.

Now stand for a moment at your own pool of tears, and
reflect on them in the light of this resurrection picture.
Weep if you need to. Allow this Easter morning scene to
deepen your belief that, on the other side of your brokenness, grief and loss, there are the possibilities of new be-

ginnings. We can look at our tears and give up in anguish and despair, or we can look up to God through them and hope for transformation. I encourage you to make the second choice. Resurrection life and tears are often interwoven. This could be why the psalmist, many centuries ago, celebrated the promise that 'those who sow in tears, will reap with songs of joy'.

Memory Verse

Those who sow in tears
will reap with songs of joy.
PSALM 126:5

TIME TO REFLECT

Describe the thoughts and feelings you experienced
while reading this chapter.

....

....

....

....

....

....

....

....

....

TAKING IT FURTHER IN
GROUP-SHARING

- *In what ways can you identify with Mary as she stands weeping outside the tomb ?*
- *What would it mean for you to look up to God through your pool of tears and hope for new beginnings?*
- *How does the message of Jesus' death and resurrection help you to befriend your tears?*

Breath-prayer

Lord, fill my life
with resurrection hope.

CHAPTER 2

Processing pain

Processing
pain

Jesus said to her, 'Woman, why are you weeping?'
(John 20:15)

One moment in my own journey through tears to transformation stands out clearly in my memory. It was 1981, and I had just taken up an appointment in a new congregation. Obviously keen to do well, I was working ten to twelve hours a day, neglecting to care for myself and often unavailable to Debbie, my new partner in marriage. Not surprisingly, I began struggling with a nagging depression that I could not get rid of. One weekend, during this period, I was the speaker at a large youth conference. After I had finished my first talk, I came down from the stage and headed for the tuckshop to buy a cool drink.

On my way a colleague, working as a psychiatrist and lecturer on the staff of a major medical school, came over and said quietly that if I ever needed to talk to someone, he would be available.

To this day I do not know what prompted that caring invitation. I can only guess that my discerning colleague perceived the hidden cry in my heart. Nonetheless, his invitation gave me the courage to phone the following week and make an appointment to see him. I remember clearly our first time together. It was a bitterly cold September day and the venue was a counselling room in a children's hospital near Johannesburg's city centre. Very kindly he had offered to see me at seven o'clock, before his working day began. As soon as I sat down I began to sob uncontrollably. I sobbed for almost half an hour. When my crying began to subside, my companion gently asked, 'Trevor, can you tell me the story that lies behind your tears?'

Looking back, I can see more clearly the importance of that question. Our tears always need to be carefully examined. Sometimes they can be sentimental or manipulative or even self-indulgent. Some of us just cry easily. My companion's question invited me to trace the source of my tears, to explore where they were coming from. As I started to talk, I began a personal journey, through tears to transformation, a journey that continues to this present day.

I was reminded of this beginning when I dug out my journal and read again what I had written about that meeting.

> 24-09-81
>
> I saw Cliff yesterday for the first time. It was an intensely painful time. I felt a physical pain in my body that I have not felt before. There were many tears. I don't know where they came from. But it was good to speak. As I heard my own words I understood a little more why I feel so much pain. It's the painful thought that if I cannot do anything for anybody I will not be acceptable to others. I wonder where this thought comes from. We made another appointment and it seems as if our relationship is going to continue.

The question was similar to the one that came to Mary, first from the angelic presences inside the tomb, and then from Jesus standing behind her. Their question was, 'Woman, why are you crying?' Notice that it is not a question that suggests judgement or condemnation. Nor is Jesus saying, 'Mary, why don't you put an end to your tears? Can't you see it is Easter Sunday morning? Pull yourself together and get on with your

life.' Rather, it is a question that invites Mary to give voice
to her pain, to bring to speech what she is experiencing, to
share the story behind her tears. It is a question that com-
municates profound respect, deep interest and warm concern. And Mary feels safe enough in Jesus' presence to
respond, 'They have taken my Lord away ... and I don't
know where they have put him' (John 20:13).

Like Mary, we need to hear that same question personally addressed to us, and offer our own personal response.
To avoid this question is to avoid our own pain. And the
consequences of trying to run away from our personal pain
are both numerous and harmful. They can range from per-
sistent depression, irrational outbursts of anger and spiritual desolation to having difficulty in touching the hearts
of others who are experiencing pain. Pain, if it is going to
end up being a positive and not a negative experience, must
be processed. It needs to find a voice and be shared. One
way to do this is to share the story behind our tears. When
we do this, we begin that sacred journey that leads us
through our tears, to transformation.

I don't think our pools of tears will ever totally dry up
this side of the grave. They may alter in size or in shape, or
change in depth, but they seldom go away completely. How-

ever, we must not give up hope.

Taking time to find someone we trust to be our 'wailing wall' and sharing the stories which our tears represent, brings immense healing benefits into our lives and relationships. Something positive and life-giving is released when our tears flow and find their voice. This could be why the church, long before the advent of modern psychology, has given special attention to 'the gift of tears'. Besides their therapeutic value which is well-documented, it is precisely at the point where we are most wounded that restorative grace and new beginnings often enter our lives. Our tears make us receptive to angelic presences and surprising resurrection encounters. It happened for Mary, and it can happen for us as well.

You may find it helpful right now, as you are reading these words, to respond to the question that came to Mary on that first Easter Sunday morning. 'Why are you crying?' In a simple prayer sentence offer your own personal response.

'Lord, I'm crying today because I'm grieving.'
'Lord, I'm crying today because my marriage is
  in pain.'

'Lord, I'm crying today because I feel like I'm in the dark.'

'Lord, I'm crying today because I don't know which way to go.'

'Lord, I'm crying today because I am far from You.'

'Lord, I'm crying today because I can't seem to find You.'

Whatever your own response may be, sharing your story around this question with the risen Lord and with a trusted listener or small group, could open the way for you to begin your journey through tears to transformation. By such sharing, you realise that you are not alone. You are connected, not only with the God who weeps with you, but also with other hurting and fragile human beings. When we become aware of these connections with God and with each other, we receive the strength and courage to live creatively, even in the midst of our pain. This is my prayer for you as you read these words.

Memory Verse

Hear my cry, O God;
Listen to my prayer.
PSALM 61:1

TIME TO REFLECT

Describe the thoughts and feelings you experienced
while reading this chapter.

. . . .
. . . .
. . . .
. . . .
. . . .
. . . .
. . . .
. . . .
. . . .

TAKING IT FURTHER IN
GROUP-SHARING

- *Describe a time in your life when someone was there for you in a time of struggle and pain.*
- *What did this person teach you about being a 'wailing wall' for others?*
- *What helps you to process pain in your own life?*

Breath-prayer

Lord, thank you that You listen
when I pour out my pain.

CHAPTER 3

Weeping with those who weep

Weeping with those who weep

Rejoice with those who rejoice; mourn with those who mourn. (Rom 12:15)

The encounter between Jesus and Mary Magdalene reminds us to take seriously one crucial New Testament ministry. It is the ministry of weeping with those who weep. This is important. It is possible to get so absorbed in our own pain, and the stories behind it, that we do not see the tears of those around us. We forget that the Risen Christ, who meets us in our tears, calls us to embody his presence in a deeply wounded world. He calls us always to follow Him, to those places where people are struggling and in need, and to share in his ministry of wiping away the tears. One way to do this is to weep with those who weep.

How, you may be wondering, can we do this? The answer is simple, but not easy to implement. We begin by learning from Jesus. What would He do if He were in our place? We watch Him take the initiative and reach out to Mary in her tears. We listen to Him asking her to put her weeping into words. We observe Him as he listens without judgement or condemnation to the story she shares. Then, in dependence on his Spirit, we learn how to follow in his footsteps with those who suffer in our midst. How to take the first step in getting closer to others in their pain. How to ask those questions that will help them to discover the voice of their tears. How to listen with respectful attention and interest to what they say. As we go about learning these ways of weeping with those who weep, we participate in the resurrection practice of wiping away the tears of others.

I witnessed this resurrection practice a few weeks ago. I was preaching in a united church in Cape Town when I noticed a man crying. After the service I saw one of the local leaders, an internationally recognised author and theologian, go across to the weeping man. I joined the rest of the congregation in another hall around tea, and about an hour later returned to the sanctuary to fetch my Bible and sermon notes. The two were still talking together, the one listening intently and the other speaking. From a distance I could see that the man had stopped crying. Later that day I had lunch with the leader and his family. I asked him about his encounter after the church service.

'What happened between you and the man who was crying?'

'I saw him sitting there weeping, so I went across, sat with him and asked if he wanted to speak,' he answered.

'Where did it go from there?'

'His story just poured out. In all my years of ministry and listening to people I have seldom come across a story of such intense pain and misery,' he told me.

'Were you able to be helpful?'

'There was nothing practical I could do,' he responded. 'But the one thing I asked was whether we could meet again for him to tell me more of his story.'

'Do you think that will help?'

'I don't know for sure. But I am convinced that new life will come when he has been able to tell his story fully to someone who will listen.'

This leader was sharing in the ministry of weeping with those who weep. Did you see how similar it was to the way Jesus reached out to Mary Magdalene in her tears? First of all, he was aware enough to look beyond himself. He was not preoccupied with his own needs, or with his own group of friends. Then, he took the initiative and approached the person in need. Next, he asked him to share his story of struggle, and listened to it. He didn't provide pat answers, or try to fix up the person with easy solutions. Rather, he gave this desperate person room to speak freely and openly about his pain. And lastly, he assured the man of his ongoing care and concern. Four simple steps, but steps that made it possible for this caring leader to become a 'wailing wall' for someone who needed one.

Ideally, this is what the church needs to be like. A community where we can come together, tell our stories, share our pain, and find hope again. If we could do this in the church, there would be far less need for the costly care of secular psychologists. However, the sad fact is that in the church we are often strangers to each other's pain. We may worship together, pray together, serve together, and yet still be totally unaware of the tears present in our sister's or brother's heart. This failure to provide room for this sharing of our painful stories is the reason why so many people leave the church, and go elsewhere to find healing and transformation for their broken lives. Often these other places are simply where people are given the opportunity to share their pain in a climate of acceptance and warmth.

But, perhaps, beginning with your and my efforts, this situation could right itself. From today onwards we can resolve to become more aware of those around us who are in pain. Almost every day people come knocking on the doors of our lives, hoping for an ear that will listen. It might be a colleague at work, a fellow team member at the club, or a brother or sister in the faith. It could even be someone with whom we live. Our calling is to simply be there, to take a caring interest, to listen to the story behind the person's tears. St Paul did not tell us to 'cheer up those who weep'; he said, 'weep with those who weep'. In other words, enter as deeply as you can into the grief and pain of your neighbour. We cannot take on the suffering of the whole world, but we can reach out to the one person near us who needs us most.

Critical as this one-to-one ministry is, however, I believe we have to take a further step. We need to forge simple structures in our groups and congregations, which facilitate the sharing of our personal stories, especially the painful ones. Each Tuesday night we try to provide this sort of climate in the little cell to which I belong. Our group consists of five families, all with teenage and young children, and all at very different stages on the Christ-following path. We often begin our evening with an invite to 'share a joy or sorrow from the past week'. I am continually struck by the ways in which this simple question facilitates story-telling and story-sharing. Community develops, not only as we share our joys, but also as we share our pain. If you belong to a small group, experiment with this question. Do not be surprised if the Risen Christ meets with your group in a special way.

Learning to weep with those who weep is a lifelong journey. I hope that this meditation has given you a glimpse of how you can share in this ministry. We must move beyond the concept of processing our personal pain, to reaching out to those others around us who are in pain. We can do this in our personal relationships. And we can create those safe and sacred spaces in our faith communities where people can share those stories that lie behind their tears. If we rise to this challenge, we become Easter people in a Good Friday world.

Memory Verse

Bear one another's burdens, and in this way
you will fulfil the law of Christ.
GALATIANS 6:2

TIME TO REFLECT

Describe the thoughts and feelings you experienced
while reading this chapter.

. . . .
. . . .
. . . .
. . . .
. . . .
. . . .
. . . .
. . . .
. . . .

TAKING IT FURTHER IN
GROUP-SHARING

- *Share one experience where you felt God used you to 'weep with those who weep'.*
- *What was this experience like for you? (Be careful not to mention the names of the people involved.)*
- *What 'human cry' in your surrounding community moves you most deeply at the moment?*

Breath-prayer

Lord, help me to connect today
with someone in pain.

CHAPTER 4

Experiencing resurrection love

Experiencing resurrection love

Jesus said to her, 'Mary!' (John 20:16)

O ne of my favourite people is Archbishop Desmond
Tutu. More than any other spiritual leader I know
in South Africa, he has constantly affirmed within the public arena the good news that each one of us is loved by
God. Recently a Sunday newspaper published an interview that Desmond had had with a journalist from the
British newspaper, *The Telegraph*. The journalist had come
to South Africa to get an Easter message for the overseas
public. As they sat together around the dining room table
in the Tutu home, Desmond spoke about his struggle with
prostate cancer, his views about the afterlife and his relationship with God. As the interview came to an end, the

journalist tells how the Archbishop stopped being the one interviewed and became instead a witness to resurrection love. He describes how Tutu, sensing that he was a lapsed Anglican, leaned across the table and, in a voice barely above a whisper, said to him, 'God loves you as you are – with your doubts, with your intellectual reservations, with your inability to make the leap of faith. God says, "I made you, actually, and I made you as you are because I love you. Don't try to titivate yourself. Just be you and know that I affirm you. You matter enormously to Me. You matter as if you were the only human being. And, you know something, I create only masterpieces. I have no doubt at all about your worth. You don't have to do anything. Your worth for Me is intrinsic. Please believe that I love you. You are not going to find ultimate satisfaction in anything out there because I made you like Me."'

I'm very aware that many people have great difficulty in personally accepting the validity of the Archbishop's words. When they look around at life, it does not seem to be penetrated by resurrection love and grace and mercy. The world seems too full of tragedy and pain for them to believe that God really cares about every human being. They think of the widespread suffering caused by earthquakes, poverty, drought, crime, injustice, acts of terrorism, and on a more personal level, illness, grief, retrenchment, depression, and they ask, 'How can there be a God who calls each one of us by name?' Perhaps even Mary Magdalene asked this question when she thought about the unfair and unjust events that had taken place on that awful Friday. So let us return again to her encounter with Jesus outside the empty tomb, and see how God's personal love came to her.

When Jesus approaches Mary from behind and asks her about her tears, she is unsure at first who it is. Thinking that he could be the gardener, she answers, 'Sir, if you have carried Him away, tell me where you have put Him, and I will get Him.' The stranger does not respond, and Mary turns away to face the tomb again. Then, from behind her, she hears a voice, simply calling, 'Mary.' Immediately she recognises the voice. It is the same voice that had addressed her with such gentleness and tenderness, when she had become accustomed to being spoken to with scorn and derision. She could never forget that voice! Now as it calls out to her, she turns with joy and cries out, 'Rabboni', a Hebrew word which means Teacher.

There are few more powerful scenes in any of the four gospels. To appreciate just a little of its poignancy, imagine yourself in Mary's place, hearing your name being called by the risen One. I once asked a small group at a retreat to do this, and then to share a brief word of response. One person responded by saying that the experience felt too good to be true. Another felt overwhelmed by joy. My own response was one of sheer wonder and amazement. How do you think you would have responded? Our imagined responses might give us a small idea of what it must have been like for Mary to hear her name being called that first Easter Sunday morning. Perhaps, if she was asked to describe the significance of this moment, she would have said something like this:

> When I heard my name being called by that familiar voice, I could hardly believe it. But it was true! Jesus, the one who had made me feel like I really mattered as a human being, and one who had given me my life back again, was alive. The love that I had experienced through his words and actions had not died with the crucifixion. His love was stronger than all the powers of evil and sin and death put together. When this truth dawned on me, I was filled with an incredible sense of joy and hope. I know for sure now that Jesus is my living teacher and friend, my mentor and Lord. I

know that there is nothing that could separate me
from his love.

Mary's experience invites us into a deeper appreciation of
what the Easter message is all about. It reminds us that, at
the heart of all things, there is a resurrection love that
seeks us passionately, calls us by name and desires a personal relationship with each one of us. Each one of us is
uniquely and individually known to the resurrected Jesus
and the God whom He reveals. When we realise this, as
Mary did, everything is changed. We do not live, as we
may have thought, in a cold, impersonal and loveless universe. We are not the insignificant and isolated individuals
that we sometimes think we are. Rather, we are eternal
creatures of infinite worth, living in a universe permeated
by brilliant rays of resurrection love and mercy and grace.

I realise that, as you read these words, you may struggle
with the reality of God's personal love. If you do, allow me
to make one simple suggestion. Take a long look at the risen
Jesus as He appears to Mary. New Testament writers have a
powerful belief that, if we want to know what God is really
like, we must look at Jesus (eg Luke 10:21–22; John 14:9;
Col 1:15). As you watch Jesus seeking Mary out and calling

her by name, imagine that ray of resurrection love piercing through Mary's tears of pain and grief. Ask the Spirit of God to help you recognise this resurrection love as it shines towards you. Usually this intimate God-love comes to us in very down to earth and ordinary ways – a loving touch, an unexpected call, a meal together, the early morning song of a bird. And if we are not alert and aware we may so easily miss it.

From personal experience, I would like to emphasise the importance of *asking* God to help us come to know and experience this resurrection love. The assurance that I am personally known, accepted and loved by God has not come easily to me. But over the years I have been learning, as I immerse myself in Gospel stories like the one with Mary, to ask God to give me an awareness of this love, not only in my head, but also in my heart. Frederick Buechner writes, 'If you have never known the power of God's love, then maybe it is because you have never *asked* to know it – I mean really asked, expecting an answer.' Almost each day I find myself asking God to open my eyes that I may see the beams of resurrection love around me in the events and experiences of my daily life. By doing this, I have been gradually discovering that our belovedness can become an inner knowing that fills our whole lives.

I hope that this meditation will help you to experience that resurrection love which lies at the heart of all things. When you do, everything changes. Your life becomes saturated with wondrous significance. You *are* known! You *are* precious! You *are* accepted! You *are* deeply loved! When you experience this good news, with your mind and heart, you find yourself taking another step through your tears to transformation. This is the good news the Archbishop tried to share with the journalist. Certainly this is the message that Mary Magdalene would want to share with you.

Memory Verse

You did not choose me
but I chose you.
JOHN 15:16

TIME TO REFLECT

Describe the thoughts and feelings you experienced
while reading this chapter.

. . . .

. . . .

. . . .

. . . .

. . . .

. . . .

. . . .

. . . .

. . . .

TAKING IT FURTHER IN
GROUP-SHARING

- *How do you respond to the Archbishop's words about God's personal love for each one of us?*
- *Describe a time when God's love touched you in a special way.*
- *How do you experience God's love in your daily life?*

Breath-prayer

Lord, help me to experience your
resurrection love today.

CHAPTER 5

*Turning
around*

Turning around

She turned … (John 20:16)

As a young person I had a very negative understanding of repentance. Whenever someone mentioned the word, a certain picture came into my mind. I remember it clearly. It was a picture of a somewhat gloomy looking man, wearing a long grey overcoat, walking down the street, and holding a sign that read, 'Repent, for the end is nigh'. To this day I do not know where this picture came from. All I do know is that I did not find this view of repentance inviting. Repentance seemed to come across more as a threat than an invitation. Not surprisingly, one of the last things I ever wanted to do was repent.

Over time I came to see repentance differently. I am thankful for this change, since repentance is one of the important themes in the message that Jesus brought. You may remember how, in his first recorded sermon, He announces, 'The time is fulfilled, and the kingdom of God has come near; repent, and believe in the good news' (Mark 1:15). Quite clearly, repentance was not something with which Jesus wanted to threaten his hearers. Rather it was an invitation for them to enter into a new kind of life. A life permeated by the immediacy of God's presence and peace and power. Repentance, supported by faith, symbolised that part which we are called to play in the drama of our own salvation. What, therefore, does this word mean?

In describing Mary's turning around to Jesus, gospel writer John provides us with a wonderful word-picture of what repentance is all about. Repentance is a translation of the Greek word *metanoia* which essentially implies a change in our way of thinking, a turning back or a turning around. It does not mean putting ourselves down, being preoccupied with our sinfulness or feeling sorry for ourselves. It may involve feeling remorse for what we have done, but it is never about earning acceptance, deserving forgiveness or trying to win God's favour. True repentance is something altogether different. It involves the complete turnaround of our mind and outlook, one that leaves us facing a new direction.

Reflect for a few moments on this picture of Mary's

'turning moment'. To begin with, notice that she turns in response to hearing her name being called. God's personal love for you and me always initiates our repentance and precedes it. Throughout our lives, indeed right from our beginnings, God is constantly seeking us, nudging us, prompting us into this change of mind and outlook. We do not earn God's love and forgiveness with our repentance. Our turning around simply enables us to experience those gifts that God wants to give us – the gifts of acceptance and mercy and new beginnings. The tragedy of not turning, is that we miss out on experiencing these life-changing treasures for ourselves.

Next, will you see that Mary turns as she is, in her grief and pain and tears. But it is a turning towards life and a fresh beginning. One of the central meanings of repentance is turning towards Jesus, as we are, and accepting the gifts of the kingdom that He freely offers us. When we turn (or return) to our Creator, we don't have to first tidy ourselves up and get everything in order. Our trust is not in our own goodness, but in the power of God's personal and intimate love to change us. That old familiar hymn puts it so well, 'Just as I am, without one plea, O Lamb of God, I come!' As we turn to Christ, our lives are touched by resurrection love, and his work of changing us from the inside begins.

Lastly, be aware that this is not the first time that Mary has turned towards Jesus. Many months previously, after He had ministered deeply to her in her brokenness, she had begun to follow Him. Mary reminds us that repentance is not a once and for all experience. Repentance is a way of life, a lifelong process of turning in a Godward direction one day at a time, that keeps our lives open to the possibilities of transformation and change. It would seem that there are many layers of consciousness within us, and on our journey towards God we constantly discover new pockets of unsurrendered self-centredness and self-interest. Such discoveries, explains Gerard Hughes, are signs of growth and progress along the spiritual way, not of failure. Christ's invitation to repent is a call to recognise these pockets of sinfulness, and to entrust ourselves anew to God's goodness and mercy.

Allow me to share how these interwoven threads of repentance have been present in my own spiritual journey. For the first sixteen years of my life, I had hardly any contact with the Christian faith. Then, when I was in Grade Ten, I met Phillip, a fellow student, who was also a Christ-follower. After a short while of friendship it became evident to me that there was something radically different about his life. It seemed as if God was very real to him, and

that this God-reality gave him a very clear sense of purpose and direction. One day I asked him about this. Very
simply he introduced me to the story of Jesus, explaining
especially how Jesus had revealed God's love through his
dying and rising. He told me that, if I wanted to experience the transforming love and power of God, I needed to
turn towards Christ and ask Him to be Lord of my life.
Late that night, walking down Havelock Street in Port Eli-
zabeth, I did this on my own, by praying a simple prayer of
personal commitment and surrender.

That was my first 'turning moment'. But it was certainly not the last. My initial 'complete surrender' was anything
but complete. Over the past thirty-four years I have had to
turn and return to God again and again, and at many different levels. Almost every day my feelings and thoughts and
actions reveal fresh layers of self-centredness and self-interest. With the help of some wonderful mentors and soul-
friends, I have been learning, when confronted with these
sinful dimensions of my life, not to berate or punish myself, but to remind myself of the incredible depths of God's
resurrection love, and to entrust myself again to Christ
'warts and all'. Only God can bring about the deep inner
transformation for which our hearts long.

Perhaps you would like to spend a few moments now

thinking about your own journey of repentance. Begin by recalling the circumstances in which you first turned towards God. Remember where you were living, what you were doing, and how God's love first came to you. Was your turning a sudden or gradual experience? Were there friends or family members who helped you turn? And since that moment how have you continued to travel along the road of repentance? Have there been other critical moments of turning? How do you sense God nudging you at the moment into a deeper surrender of yourself? It would be wonderful if, as you finish reading this meditation, you entered into a deepened experience of repentance. It could open your life to a renewed experience of resurrection life.

Memory Verse

Do you not realise that God's kindness
is meant to lead you to repentance?
ROMANS 2:4

TIME TO REFLECT

Describe the thoughts and feelings you experienced
while reading this chapter.

. . . .

. . . .

. . . .

. . . .

. . . .

. . . .

. . . .

. . . .

. . . .

TAKING IT FURTHER IN
GROUP-SHARING

- *Can you describe your first 'turning moment' to God?*
- *How do you experience God when you turn towards Him?*
- *In what ways do you sense God nudging you into a deeper repentance?*

Breath-prayer

Lord, help me to turn and yield
myself to You afresh.

r

Becoming a learner of Jesus

Becoming a learner of Jesus

She turned towards him and cried out in Aramaic,
'Rabboni!' (which means Teacher) (John 20:16)

Recently I undertook some further studies. Becoming a student again in my fifties was quite a challenge. Nonetheless, it was a time of new learning and expanding my horizons. One of the things that became clear for me again was how so much of our knowledge about life comes from other people. Whether it be from our parents, our schoolteachers, our pastors, our peers, our bosses at work or Oprah Winfrey on TV, throughout our lives we are constantly learning from others how to live. Even when we claim that we make up our own minds, we often do so because someone has suggested it to us. In a nutshell, we are always someone's disciple to some degree or another.

One of the most revealing moments in our lives occurs when we begin to reflect on who our most significant teachers have been and when we critically examine the effects that their words and actions have had on our lives. When these effects have been life-giving and creative, we have much to give thanks for. Sadly, sometimes these ideas about life that we have gotten from others may have not worked in our favour. They may even have done much damage and caused much heartache. The good news, however, is that the process of learning how to live never ends. We can always choose again whose disciple we want to be.

Mary Magdalene was clear about whose disciple she wanted to be. When she turned towards Jesus, she called out, 'Teacher!' By using this word she gave us a glimpse of what her relationship with Jesus meant to her. Besides being her dearest friend and life-giving deliverer, He was also her beloved 'rabbi' whose words had illuminated her life. He had helped her to make sense of her world and given her new purpose and direction. His teachings had shown her how to build her life upon a rock. Now his victory over death gave eternal validity to his words. By raising Him from the grave, God had underlined Jesus' teachings with divine authority. Whatever the future of their relationship would be, Mary somehow wanted to remain a learner in the company of Jesus. She instinctively expressed this deep desire with her exclamation, 'Teacher!'

In this word Mary reminds us that, when we turn towards Christ, we do well to come as learners. After all, our repentance makes us citizens of a radically different new kingdom, a kingdom where the last are first, the weak are strong and leaders are servants first. We will want to learn all we can about this strange kingdom, and how we can participate in it. There is a new language for us to learn – the language of self-giving and sacrificial love. There is a family history to make our own – a history of God's people stretching from biblical times right into the present. There are new habits to adopt – habits of worship and prayer, life-sharing and servanthood, giving and receiving. Following Jesus as learners ushers us into this different kingdom, opens our hearts to the power of the Spirit and gradually transforms our character into God's family likeness.

How, then, do you and I become learners of Jesus? Obviously it cannot mean trying to become carbon-copies of his Palestinian life with its sandals and robes. It would not make sense for us to try to live the kind of life Jesus lived two thousand years ago. If you are like me, part of a family living in the modern world, consider some of the differences between our lives and his. Jesus was not married, did not have children, didn't drive on congested highways to work each morning and was not faced with the particular challenges of nation-building with which we need to contend in South Africa today. There is just no way in which we can try to copy Jesus' historical life. We cannot uproot ourselves from our present lives as spouses, parents, highway commuters or a world of high technology and social complexity and imitate Jesus in his cultural and social setting.

Nor, I dare suggest, does it mean constantly asking ourselves, 'What would Jesus do in my present situation?' There is of course nothing wrong with asking the WWJD question. But in many cases we already know what Jesus would do. The problem is that, regardless of what we think Jesus would do, we often end up doing what our nature and habits have trained us to do. What is in us, instinctively comes out. The crucial challenge facing us, therefore, involves learning from Jesus how to become within ourselves the kind of person who will naturally and habitually embody how He would respond in any given situation. To put it simply, we need to let Christ, our living teacher, transform us from within, changing our habits and automatic responses in the reality of this present world.

This inner transformation of the 'command centre' of

our being happens as we embark on a learning journey with rabbi Jesus, alive and present in our midst. We ask the ever-living Christ to be our teacher, immerse ourselves in his life, allow his words to shape us inwardly and live out of his revelation as faithfully as we can.

This adventure will seldom be straightforward or neat and tidy. Discipleship, like life, is messy, complex and difficult. Nonetheless, as we yoke ourselves to Jesus in the way described above, we do begin to live differently. We find ourselves living with different attitudes, different words and different behaviours. Over time we sense that we are becoming new people, developing Christlike habits and Christlike responses that become part of our nature, and that we don't have to think too much about. Amazingly, we learn from our own experience that Christ can be our living teacher, just as he was for Mary on that first Easter Sunday morning.

If you really want to become a learner of Jesus, may I invite you into this experiment. Set aside a few months to read one of the gospels slowly. Perhaps you could start with the Gospel of Mark. Soak yourself in those words the gospel writer gives as coming from Jesus Himself. Let his words form you, shape you, challenge you. Let the phrases seep deeply into your heart and mind. Don't rush the process, saying to yourself that you have read all these words before. Take time to pray what you read into your place of work, your home, your relationships, your hopes for the future. Ask the Lord to make his Word and his Spirit come alive in your heart, so that you may see your daily life through his eyes, lit with the light of the word which He has spoken to you.

As you go about this immersion of yourself in Mark's gospel, learn to live your life as Christ would if He were in your place. Seek the help and power of God's Spirit. Improvise, with the help of others, in your relationships, in your work, in your town, a life of faith, hope and compassionate caring. In time you will sense God changing you from the inside out, helping you to respond to the conditions of your life differently. You will gradually find yourself living with different habits, different attitudes, different words, different behaviours. You will also discover – and this is a wonderful gift of grace – that you are not alone. Jesus, in the power of his Spirit, steps out of the pages of the Gospel and becomes an empowering presence and close companion in the daily experience of your life.

Follow Mary's example and become a learner of Jesus. You will discover life at its best!

Memory Verse

Take my yoke upon you, and learn from me,
for I am gentle and humble in heart,
and you will find rest for your souls.
MATTHEW 11:29

TIME TO REFLECT

Describe the thoughts and feelings you experienced
while reading this chapter.

. . . .

. . . .

. . . .

. . . .

. . . .

. . . .

. . . .

. . . .

. . . .

TAKING IT FURTHER IN
GROUP-SHARING

- *Describe the influence of one significant person upon your life.*
- *In what ways has Christ been your living teacher?*
- *In what specific area of your present life experience do you need the guidance of Christ?*

Breath-prayer

Lord, teach me
how to be your disciple.

CHAPTER 7

*Letting go
and letting God*

Letting go and letting God

Jesus said, 'Do not hold on to me, ...' (John 20:17)

There is a story of the man who was climbing the mountain when he lost his balance and fell. Just as he was going over the edge of the cliff, he grabbed hold of a small branch and held on for dear life. Swinging there over the abyss, he prayed, 'Oh God help me.'

A gentle voice answered, 'Do you trust Me?'

'You know I trust You, Lord, that's why I'm speaking to You.'

The voice asked again, 'Do you trust Me?'

'Yes Lord, of course I trust You.'

This time the voice came back loudly, 'Then let go.'

There is of course another rather naughty ending to

the story where the man says, 'Is there anyone else up there I can speak to?'

Seriously though, if we want to experience God's peace and power at a deeper level, we need to learn to let go. This does not mean becoming passive, or inactive, or irresponsible. Nor does it mean saying 'what will be will be' in a spirit of resignation. Letting go is an act of true surrender. No longer do we insist on having everything go our way. We let go of the I, me and mine. We give up sitting on the throne of our life, and allow Christ to become our Lord. We align our will with God's viewpoint and begin seeking God's way for our everyday life. Taking the risk of letting go, of entrusting ourselves to God, lies at the heart of personal transformation. The more we trust, the more we let God be God, the more free we become.

I believe this is what Mary Magdalene began to discover on that resurrection morning. Go back for a moment to those words which Jesus spoke to her, 'Don't hold onto Me'. At first glance they seem a little uncaring. They must surely have pierced her heart. The past two nights had probably been the darkest of her life. She had gone through heartache and desolation. She thought she would never see Jesus again, or hear his voice, or feel his touch. As she recognised Him, in this moment, and realised that He was alive, one can understand her instinctive need to throw her arms around Him. To never let go of Him again. Yet Jesus does not want her to do this.

In reality, Jesus is not being insensitive. He is inviting Mary into a new level in their relationship. Jesus, the one who comforts, now becomes the one who challenges. His command is crisp and clear. He asks Mary not to cling to Him. He wants her to learn to let go and let God. To open her hands. To trust.

You see, Jesus has deeper intentions for Mary's life. He does not want her to remain a clinger all her life. He knows that clinging shrinks the soul, undermines trust and impedes the growth of a transforming friendship with God. And so He yearns for her to open her clenched fists, and to become a person who is able to let go. If she really desires to continue her journey towards transformation, she must be set free from the need to cling and learn to let go. And so He commands her, 'Don't hold onto Me.' It's the invitation of love, the challenge of radical trust, asking for open hands.

Those who belong to Alcoholics Anonymous express beautifully what Jesus is asking Mary to do here. They speak of how important it is 'to let go and let God'. This slogan underlines how vital it is to surrender all of our certainties, to entrust ourselves completely to God, to be willing to let God be God in our lives. From his own experience Jesus knows the peace and power that comes when we do this. Hours before He was crucified He prayed in Gethsemane the prayer of someone who knew what it meant to let go, 'Father, not my will but yours be done.' He wants Mary to enter into that same deep experience of trusting, surrender and letting go.

The decision to let go and let God is not something we do once and for all. Our initial surrender to Christ allows Him, as it were, entrance through the front door of our house. It expresses our willingness to let God transform, if necessary, the whole of our personal, sexual, financial and social lives. But it is only the beginning of the faith journey. In order to live fully in the house of transformation, we need to turn over to Christ, room by room, every aspect of our personalities, especially those rooms hidden from public view. As we do this, we learn that conversion is a life-long process that takes place gradually, one day at a time.

I need to emphasise also that this process of letting go can be a real struggle. That part of us that wants to be at the centre, to be in control, to have life work out 'our way' constantly tries to get back on the throne of our lives. We can surrender our whole lives to God first thing in the morning. But an hour later we can find ourselves sick with worry about some aspect of our work, or about our finances, or about the future of our country. We can entrust our loved ones to God and pray that they will become all that God wants them to be. But within minutes we can find ourselves telling them how they should be running their lives. As we catch ourselves doing this, all we can do is to gently return to Christ, express again our willingness to let go and to let God, and ask God to continue to guide us as the day goes along.

As you end this meditation, I invite you to share in a brief exercise. It is one that I do again and again. Wherever you may be sitting now, make yourself comfortable and place your hands upon your lap. Curl up your fingers into tightly closed fists. Imagine that in these tightly clenched hands you are holding onto everything that is important for you – your life, your loved ones, your work, your possessions, your resentments, your hopes and dreams for the future. Feel the tension build up from your hands. Now hear the invitation from Christ to let go and let God. It is an invitation to deeper surrender and yieldedness. As you are able, allow your response to find expression in the slow opening of your hands.

May you know the joy and serenity that comes from letting go and letting God!

Memory Verse

Father into your hands
I commit my spirit.
LUKE 23:46

TIME TO REFLECT

*Describe the thoughts and feelings you experienced
while reading this chapter.*

. . . .
. . . .
. . . .
. . . .
. . . .
. . . .
. . . .
. . . .
. . . .

TAKING IT FURTHER IN
GROUP-SHARING

- *How do you respond to the word 'surrender'?*
- *What has helped you to deepen your trust in God?*
- *How are you needing to 'let go and let God' at the moment?*

Breath-prayer

Lord, help me to live
with open hands.

CHAPTER 8

*Giving space
to loved ones*

Giving space to loved ones

Jesus said, 'Do not hold on to me, for I have not
yet returned to the Father.' (John 20:17)

A few months ago, I watched my eighteen year old
daughter walk away from me through the departure
lounge of the Johannesburg Airport. She was on her way
to board a South African Airways plane bound for Lon-
don. She had been planning this trip for several years and
had saved every cent she could. It was going to be a two
month holiday during which she hoped to listen to her
favourite 'punk' bands, visit some art galleries and experience life in another country. It was also her first time
away from home for any length of time.

As she turned to wave goodbye, I felt conflicting emo-

tions. On the one hand, I was happy for her. She was growing up, leaving behind her childhood dependencies and
beginning to explore life on her own. I wanted her to
know that she was going with my full blessing. In spoken
and unspoken ways, in the days prior to her leaving, I had
tried to convey the message: 'I love you, I trust you, I am
proud of you and send you off freely. You are my deeply
beloved daughter and I delight in you.'

But on the other hand, I was not finding it easy to let
go. Whilst I knew with my head that it was important to
start giving her freedom, a part of me still longed for those
days when she would sit on my lap and uncritically take in
everything I said. Those times, however, were long gone. I
knew that I needed to put behind me the way I used to
relate to her. I knew that I needed to learn to connect with
my daughter in a new way, that would give her more space
and allow her the freedom to become more of the person
she wanted to be.

The widely read spiritual writer Henri Nouwen has point-
ed out that real intimacy involves both closeness and distance. Finding the balance, however, can be quite difficult.
Sometimes we need to be held and hugged. At other times
we need the space to move freely. What makes matters even
more tricky is that usually the needs of the two people in

a relationship are quite different at any one given moment. One person may need closeness while the other wants distance. One might want to be held while the other needs space. In spite of these difficulties, however, if we honestly try to discern when to come close or when to allow space, it can often open up our closest relationships to new growth and much deeper intimacy.

It seems that Mary Magdalene was the kind of person who found it easier to hold on to loved ones than to give them space. So Jesus wants her now to open herself to a new spacious intimacy in their relationship. He encourages her in this direction by assuring her that, as the ascended Lord, his spiritual presence will be present throughout the universe. Wherever Mary goes, whatever she does, He will be with her. There is nothing that will ever separate her from his resurrection love and presence. Therefore she must stop clinging to Him. 'Do not hold onto Me,' He says to her, 'because I have not yet ascended to the Father.'

Perhaps we also find it difficult to give space to our loved ones. Often in our close relationships we try to possess and hold on to one another. We do this because we need security or because it gives us a false sense that we are in control and in charge of what happens. It could also be that our need to be loved is so great that, when someone does show us some affection and caring, we are inclined to cling to them. We demand more from them than they are able to give. As a result, many people feel suffocated in their relationships. They feel they are not being given enough freedom to breathe, to live, to move. As someone said to me in a marriage counselling interview recently, 'I just need some space to be my own person.'

God's relationship with each of us gives us a wonderful model of spacious intimacy. Have you ever noticed that God is seldom pushy? I cannot speak for you, but I have personally never experienced the divine presence forcing itself on me. Nor have I ever known God to coerce or pressurise me into a particular course of action. The gift of God's personal love is always freely offered and we are free to respond in our own way. Similarly, the way the Spirit moves in our hearts and minds is usually quiet, gentle and inviting. It is never forced on us. For this reason we are often able to avoid or explain away God's loving overtures towards us. And when we do, God rarely responds with fire from heaven. More likely God simply gives us the space to continue our lives as we choose.

In the same way that God relates to us, we need also to relate to others. On the one hand, we really want to be able to express our love and care for them. On the other hand, we should do this without holding on to them. We need to gradually learn how to take our hands off of their lives. This is what it means to give space to our loved ones. In effect, when we let them go in this way, we are saying to them something like this:

> I believe that you were created to live freely.
> I place your life into the loving hands of your Creator.
> I let go of my clinging hold on your life.
> I am willing for you to make your own choices.
> I no longer want to play god in your life.
> I will not believe that I always know what is best for your life.
> I want you to live your own life according to your best understanding and light.
> I respect the image of God in you.
> I want to learn to love you with open hands.
> I love you and I bless you. I have confidence in you and always will.

Right now, you may like to say these words aloud on behalf of a specific loved one you would like to think about. This person may be struggling with alcohol or substance abuse, or making choices with which you disagree, or refusing to respond to your gestures of love and affection in the way you would like. Notice how these affirmations affect your interactions with this person. Wait on God, and see how God's Spirit works in your relationship. It could be that you are surprised by a little Easter. Just about any time we experience new possibilities for life and healing in our close relationships, there is a little Easter that happens that gives us a glimpse of the power of resurrection love. May this happen for you in the days ahead.

Memory Verse

No one has greater love than this,
to lay down one's life for one's friends.
JOHN 15:13

TIME TO REFLECT

*Describe the thoughts and feelings you experienced
while reading this chapter.*

. . . .

. . . .

. . . .

. . . .

. . . .

. . . .

. . . .

. . . .

. . . .

TAKING IT FURTHER IN
GROUP-SHARING

- *Describe a time when you needed to give space to a loved one.*
- *What helps you to give space to loved ones?*
- *How do you sense God calling you at the moment to deepen intimacy in your close relationships?*

Breath-prayer

Lord, I place my loved ones
in your hands.

CHAPTER 9

Sharing
the message

Sharing the message

Go instead to my brothers and tell them, 'I am returning to my Father and your Father, to my God and your God.' Mary Magdalene went to the disciples with the news: 'I have seen the Lord!' And she told them that he had said these things to her. (John 20:17–18)

Over the past few years I have learnt a great deal from my friends who attend Alcoholics Anonymous. They often tell me about the twelve-step programme that they are seeking to follow. Few other programmes have brought as much healing and transformation into people's lives as this one. Built into this life-saving programme is the necessity to pass on the message of hope and recovery. The twelfth step reads, 'Having had a spiritual awakening as a result of these steps, we try to carry this message to others and to practise these principles in all our affairs'. Implied in this step is the belief that, in order for the recovering alcoholic to stay on the road to recovery, he or she must share what they have received.

I believe that this principle also holds true for those who are wanting to follow Christ. We need to pass on the good news that has touched our lives. When we do this, our faith continues to grow and deepen. When we don't, it often shrivels up and dies. This could be why my prayer counsellor, on the night of my first public commitment to Jesus, insisted, 'Trevor, please make sure that you tell someone as soon as you can about the step that you have taken tonight.' He must have known that sharing Christ with others makes Him more real to us as well.

But we don't only share our faith because it keeps us spiritually alive. We share our faith because Jesus insists that we do. We see this clearly in the final moments of his gospel encounter with Mary Magdalene. Their time together comes to an end with Jesus challenging Mary to go and share the news of his resurrection with his disciples. Still living in the darkness of Good Friday, they need to receive the wonderful news of resurrection hope and light. Jesus knows this and he wants Mary to be the bearer of this message.

Her response is immediate. She runs to the disciples and tells them, 'I have seen the Lord.' Will you note that she does not tell the disciples what they ought to believe or do. Nor does she engage in any kind of theological argument or discussion. She simply tells her story. She has personally seen Jesus with the eyes of faith and knows that his living presence will always be with her. So immediately the power of the resurrection begins to flow through her to others. She becomes an Easter person living in a Good Friday world.

The Living One continues to call you and me to be Easter people in a Good Friday world. As He did with Mary, Jesus calls us to go to the dark places of our world, which are marked by the signs of crucifixion. He calls us to where our neighbours and friends live in the darkness of despair and loneliness. He calls us into those communities where poverty, homelessness and crime block out the sunlight. He calls us to descend into those dark pits where people feel cut off and abandoned by God. In all these dark places, his challenge remains the same. We must listen to the stories of those who suffer. Wipe away the tears. Share with others our own personal experience of the Easter message.

How do we pass on this Easter message? Certainly not by trying to force others to believe in exactly the same way that we do. Nor by attempting 'to fix up' those around us with our solutions and prescriptions for their lives. Mary teaches us that the best way to be a witness is by simply sharing our personal story. By telling others how the living Christ has shone the light in our darkness. By explaining the difference that 'letting go and letting God' has made to our lives. By testifying how our lives have been touched by resurrection love. And to always do this with gentleness, respect and courtesy. I think it was DT Niles who once said that passing on the good news is like 'one beggar telling another beggar where he or she can find some bread'.

Usually our opportunities to share our personal experiences of God only come *after* we have tried to get to know people on their own terms. This means being interested in them and what they are going through, instead of trying to look for gaps to speak about our spiritual pilgrimage. I am aware that this may sound contradictory to the usual ideas associated with 'spreading the Word'. But I have learnt over the years that usually our best witness to God's personal love consists of keeping quiet, and listening before we talk. When we listen before we speak, we get a much better hearing.

If you want to experiment with what I am suggesting, go from reading of this passage and ask someone with whom you either live or work how they are doing. Listen and show an active interest in what they tell you. I'm sure that they will sense that you've changed a bit and they may even want to know why!

A recent conversation brought home for me again how important it is to be interested in others if one wants to be a witness. At a wedding reception I was seated alongside a rather impressive looking man. We introduced ourselves and I learnt that he was a doctor working in the same city where I worked. He asked me what I did for a living. I told him that I was a pastor of a local congregation. When he heard this he told me that he was not a religious man, did not go to church and no longer believed in God. I was genuinely intrigued in what he said and tried to show my interest.

'Can you tell me about this God in whom you don't believe,' I enquired.

'Certainly,' he answered. 'I don't believe at all in a God who sits somewhere up in the sky and controls everything that happens like a puppet master.'

'That's interesting,' I replied. 'Neither do I.'

'What kind of God do you believe in?' he asked.

What followed was an exceptionally meaningful conversation. Not only did I learn more of where this man's notions about God had come from, but he also shared at length his previous experiences with the church, some of which had been quite painful. In response to his interest I was able to share that for me God was not some distant figure, but rather a living and active presence with, within and around me. I told him briefly about some of the strengthening effects that my relationship with God had brought into my life, especially in times of struggle and difficulty. I wish I could say that our conversation had ended with him asking me how to get to know God but it didn't. His last words to me were, 'Well, you never know, you may see me in church one of these days.'

You may be wondering at this point just what you would say if the opportunity came for you to share your experience of God. Perhaps I could ask you to do a simple exercise that may help you to find the words to tell your own faith-story. Begin by thinking about a real-life problem that you have had to recently deal with in some area of your life. It may have been a difficulty in your marriage, a crisis at work, a financial struggle, a battle with depression or something else that is quite personal. Ask yourself how your relationship with the Risen Christ made a difference to the way you responded to this problem. Write down your response.

When you have completed the exercise, you have the beginnings of your own up-to-date Easter story at hand, ready to be shared.

Memory Verse

But you will receive power
when the Holy Spirit comes on you;
and you will be my witnesses …
ACTS 1:8

TIME TO REFLECT

*Describe the thoughts and feelings you experienced
while reading this chapter.*

....
....
....
....
....
....
....
....
....

TAKING IT FURTHER IN
GROUP-SHARING

- *Who was the first person to share the message of Christ with you?*
- *How do you feel talking about your faith?*
- *Share a recent experience where the Risen Christ helped you face a difficult problem.*

Breath-prayer

Lord, help me to be your witness today.

CHAPTER 10

Exploring our
living hope

Exploring our living hope

> Blessed be the God and Father of our Lord Jesus Christ! By his great mercy he has given us a new birth into a living hope through the resurrection of Jesus Christ from the dead ... (1 Pet 1:3)

Let me be open and honest with you. I have deeply conflicting reactions to death. There is a huge part of me that really loves life and enjoys the good things of this physical world, and wants to delay my departure from it for as long as possible. This part of me does not enjoy thinking about death, especially my own or the death of those close to me. The death of my father some years ago left a lot of pain in my heart that continues until today.

There is another part of me that does want to face the issue of death and think seriously about its consequences. As I get older I find my thoughts drawn to the subject more and more. What will it be like? What lies beyond? How can I face it with dignity and without fear? Will I be able to recognise those that I have loved? The questions go on and on.

However, I have found that there are not many people around with whom one can honestly share one's feelings about death. It is a subject most people tend to want to avoid. Our generation is afraid of many things, but it fears few things more than it does death. Can you imagine the next time you attend a dinner party, or share a meal with your friends at a restaurant, asking those you are with, 'What do you feel and think about death?' It is likely that your question will cause a fair degree of discomfort and unease. A real wet blanket!

One reason for this avoidance is the strongly materialistic outlook of our day and age. Our lives have been powerfully shaped by a culture that focuses on the physical. We are strongly tempted to believe that the only things that are real in life are those things that we can taste and see and smell and touch. Therefore, when we consider the possibility of our bodies decomposing when we die, there is a deep-rooted feeling that this actually could be the end of our existence.

How incredibly different must Mary Magdalene's attitude towards death have been, after her encounter with the Risen Christ. On that Easter morning when she found the tomb empty, heard her name being called and discovered that Jesus was alive, her heart must have been filled with an amazing feeling of hope. The love which Jesus had shown her, the love which He had lived, the love which He embodied had not been defeated by the dark power of death. I can almost picture her running back to the disciples with a new song in her heart. Death was not the end. Jesus her Lord was alive again, living beyond a terrible crucifixion in a completely new and transformed way!

And how do you think the disciples responded when she arrived at their door with the news, 'I have seen the Lord'? Did they smile knowingly, thinking to themselves that Mary may have cracked under the pressure? Did they wonder whether she was hallucinating? Or did they look at each other with the subtle fear that sometimes comes to us in those moments when we become aware that the world is not as we think it is? Whatever their reaction may have been, it probably did not bother Mary too much. She had personally experienced the living presence of Jesus. She knew that there was now nothing left to fear, not even the terrible reality of death.

As followers of Jesus we are invited to share in Mary's living hope and allow 'resurrection possibilities' into our dark situations. Through the centuries the attitude of Christ followers towards death for example has been in marked contrast to the attitudes of others around them. Remember how the early Christian martyrs went to their death in the Colosseum singing and praising, even blessing those who had sentenced them to death. They were not play-acting. They were living out of their confident assurance that their relationship with Christ, begun in this life, would continue in an ever richer and fuller way. They knew that their death was a doorway into a new dimension of life in an eternal kingdom. They knew they were safe.

Having a living hope does not mean that we do have unrealistic attitudes to trouble and suffering, or that we do not experience deep grief when a loved one dies. Of course, we feel these things and the awful pain and anguish that comes when we can no longer touch someone we have loved deeply. We cry, we grieve, we hurt like anyone else. Sometimes we might even shake our fists at God wondering how this could have been allowed to happen. Especially when we lose a child. And if we have only built our lives and our hopes entirely on our loved ones, then our joy will always be a fragile thing. But if our deepest confidence is in the God who raised Jesus from the dead, then our sadness will not be trapped in hopelessness and despair. We will be able to grieve with hope.

Can you now see why the most important challenge facing us in this life is to grow our relationship with the Risen Christ and the God whom He reveals? Nothing is more important. The practical aspects of how we do this is not the central theme of this book, but let me just very briefly note a few things that I have found helpful in my own pilgrimage. Here they are.

- *We can think deeply about the resurrection narratives of Jesus. These stories remind us that the final word about our lives belongs to God and not death. They help us to see that there is far more to this universe than what meets the eye.*
- *We can get to know all we can about Jesus of Nazareth by reading and re-reading the four gospels. Once our lives have been touched by his resurrected presence, He becomes for us the Way, the Truth and the Life. As we learn to follow Him, He steps out of the Gospel and becomes a living presence for us.*
- *We can share regularly together with other worshippers in Holy Communion. As we take the broken bread, and drink the*

wine, the risen Lord renews our faith and our hope in Him.

- *We can shape our lives and actions to reflect the pattern of Jesus' unconditional love for us. This is always the acid test of whether our lives have been touched by the living Jesus or not: are we growing in our ability to love the people around us in the same way that Christ has loved us?*
- *We can keep our hope alive in all the situations we face, even death and dying. This will take decision and determination. We must courageously turn our faces away from worry, fear and cynicism and choose to be people of hope. As we consciously lean on our risen Lord and Friend in tough situations, we will be given the inner resources to do this in amazing ways.*

In closing – Mary's encounter with the risen Jesus on that first Easter Sunday morning shows us how his resurrection can give birth to a living hope in our lives. A living hope that our pools of tears can actually become opportunities for transformation and growth. A living hope that reminds us that at the heart of all things, there is a resurrection love that will never let us go. Above all, it is a living hope that even death cannot take away and which enables us to cry out with all those who have gone before us, 'Where, O death, is your victory? Where, O death, is your sting?' (1 Cor 15:55).

Memory Verse

Be joyful in hope,
patient in affliction,
faithful in prayer.
ROMANS 12:12

TIME TO REFLECT

*Describe the thoughts and feelings you experienced
while reading this chapter.*

. . . .
. . . .
. . . .
. . . .
. . . .
. . . .
. . . .
. . . .
. . . .
. . . .

TAKING IT FURTHER IN
GROUP-SHARING

- *What are your thoughts and feelings about death and dying?*
- *What role does hope play in your life?*
- *How can you practically deepen your relationship with the Risen Christ?*

Breath-prayer

Lord, be my living hope today.